D1096722

# Oracle Guide
# For Your Ascension Journey

## Channeled Messages Complemented with Energy Transmission

### Book One

*by Zouza Wakinyan*

Copyright © 2021 by Zouza Wakinyan
All rights reserved.
Cover Art Illustration © by vanilladesign at Dreamstime.com
Owl Image by Chraecker at pixabay.com
ISBN 978-0-578-91675-0

# Contents

# How to Use This Book

The vibrationally channeled messages within this book, along with the scanning of the kabbalistic symbol as shown below, can assist and guide those who resonate with it.

See if this book is right for you! Take a deep breath to calm and silence your mind as much as possible, then focus your attention into your heart center. When you feel ready, just open the book to a page you instinctively choose. Don't second guess yourself. Read the story you open to without trying to intellectualize it; simply allow its transmission to flow through you. Pay attention to how you feel, and especially take note if you receive a message that seems connected to any experience or situation in your current life. Does it speak to you or to your senses? You (and only you) will know if it is a fit, and if so, what reflection is there for you.

This book was not channeled in a manner to be read linearly, although you could read it that way if you choose. It is not necessarily a book you open every day, but whenever you feel a strong call to do so. Whenever you need assistance, open it. You will find that the message you land on will be the right one for you in that moment. Try not to force its guidance, as you may find that you will not receive what you want. The passages are meant to give you what you need, when you need it.

Inserted throughout the book are several Kabbalistic symbols, from those known as the "72 Names of God". This is a symbolistic light technology that your soul will recognize.

You can read the associated meditation while scanning the symbols from right to left for as long as you wish.

Unconditional love to You!

~ *Zouza Wakinyan*

*Scan from right to left*

## Appreciation

*With the power of this name, I access the infinite abundance from Source and bring it into this present moment and embodiment from which I am emanating a state of abundance and appreciation for myself and everything else with a deep sense and knowing that I am enough as I am Now.*

# Note for the Reader

I dedicate this book to all of you who have the intrepidity to engage on this journey of evolutionary transformation on Earth.

This evolutionary process, which many call ascension, is in its most basic form the process of transcending duality through the perfection of a balancing act between polarities: dark / light, feminine / masculine, positive / negative. The key and power of this process resides in the gift of every present moment, which can be accessed through conscious awareness.

Prior to ascension there is an awakening taking place which, in my view, is an awareness of our dream or existence in the multi-dimensional time and space.

For ascension to occur, one must be able to achieve and maintain a higher vibrational state. There are many paths to this state of being, and I will mention some I personally have come to realize:

- Following your passion and joy as often as possible

- Maintaining a neutral observer state of being

- Mastering your own specific and desired vibrational frequency

- Cultivating joy and love in your very existence

- Following the path of least resistance

- Living in the heart

Ascension does not mean physically traveling to another time and space, although it may magically feel like it! And as many of us come to discover, the process of ascension is not a journey into the light or an upwards journey only, it is also a journey downwards into our darkness. This is often explained using the analogy of the "rubber band effect": the more you stretch yourself into the darkness, the more you will be able to reach farther into the light due to the universal natural laws of rhythm and balance, which will always prevail.

Your heart exists in unity, a crystallized perfect balance between opposites. That is why, I believe, ascension is essentially a journey into your heart. Your physical mind exists in duality, and that is why all that is created through only the mind will contain both the positive and the negative, as separate creations coexisting together. Create from your heart-based structure, then use your mind as an "executive branch" to direct and focus your heart-centered commands.

I have come to realize that ascension is a unique and individual process. One can illuminate many paths yet not instruct on the attainment. I was told by the light being which communicated these messages to me, that these channeled messages can be used as a guide during this transitional phase of ascension and will help you create a bridge between the physical and the nonphysical. I, myself, use the messages this way. This connection can act as a grounding rod as you go through your process, which will help elevate your physical, spiritual, and mental bodies. Use this book as a fast-track, easy access gateway to the heart!

If I am to assess my Earth transformational journey so far, I would say that the most important task is to continually remind myself to refocus on staying aware and present, especially in difficult or dark times.

Here are some inalienable truths I was taught during my own transformational process so far:

- You are never alone. Powerful and evolved nonphysical loving beings are always around you.

- You are loved and supported unconditionally, regardless of your mistakes and missteps.

- You are the center of your universe and absolutely nothing can happen to you unless you agree to it at some level. Fear, for instance, is an agreement to attract and experience that-which you believe is more powerful than you. Confront and inquire into your fears always.

- Your core belief system is what originates your reality creation! Your *beliefs* determine your unique *perception* of reality which is further influencing your *thoughts*. *Thoughts*, like everything in the universe, have a specific vibration and therefore generate specific *emotions* which prompt you to take certain *actions*. This is the complex process through which you create your reality. Honest, self-inquiry into your belief system is key to your creation process.

- You are the Light, You are the Dark, and You are always in control of your own reality. It is in your power to create anything you desire.

- You are always manifesting what you need (consciously or unconsciously) in order to move to the next level.

- You are exactly where you need to be in every single moment of your existence, as the universal vibrational law of attraction makes no mistakes. Face your present circumstances with conscious awareness.

- Your inner world is always reflected in your outer world. Acknowledge the clues presented in your outer world. Be present and accept the responsibility of your part in the co-creation of reality by taking any action available to you, so you can create the reality that resonates with your heart-song. Act as if it is already there!

*Remember to always follow your Joy!*

# Abyss and Absence

Expansion of consciousness is an automatic process generated by the action of sinking into the abyss of your own existence. The deeper you dive in, the more your consciousness is expanding. This is a truth which humanity needs to understand at this time. However, the enlightenment resides somewhere else.

What is the abyss you are diving into? What is that you signed up for? Where does it take you?

Dear One, there is just "Void" which is basically an absence of everything. It is your empty "canvas".

Dear children o light, filling the Void is a choice of every single one of you and all of you together. It is a choice and a responsibility and, therefore, we are suggesting you choose wisely and take responsibility for every choice you make. We are aware you know this, and yet we are choosing to repeat it one last time for you: *choose wisely and take responsibility* for your creation!

*Scan from right to left*

## Heaven on Earth

*With the power of this name, I ignite the divine light within myself as guidance of my own transformation and therefore I become a channel for divine creation of a true Heaven on Earth!*

# Ambition and Resemblance

History relates many events where ambitious minds were attempting to reach the impossible. There are cases where the impossible may not have been reached, but certainly a door or many were opened.

The main reason why ambition in itself is not enough to reach a certain goal is the fact that the human mind is mainly a resilient one. It tends to look back for reference or confirmation.

When the impossible is being targeted, you cannot validate it by using past references. The past will limit you to what it was, while the future will free you to the infinite possibilities of what you can imagine.

Do not limit yourself to what you can see or remember, but instead, free yourself to what you can imagine!

*Scan from right to left* ←

## Reveal the Dark Side

*With the power of this name,*
*I use the alchemy of life to reveal and transform*
*negativity within myself, now and forever!*

# Appearance of the Dark

How dark is being perceived by one entity depends on that entity's specific experiences and uniqueness. Darkness can take many forms and often is disguised and appears as illusory light.

How would one distinguish between darkness and light or between true light and illusory light? This is a challenge of the Heart!

Light is perceived by One's heart in a unique and undoubtable way. This is the fine-tuning of light frequencies as you approach higher levels of consciousness.

The true challenge is in fact not to distinguish between someone else's light and darkness, but to recognize it in yourself and therefore distinguish between your own light and darkness. Unconsciously, your ego tends to often disguise your darkness as illusory light.

The key to a successful discernment process is total and complete surrender and trust in your own life process. Knowing that you are always at the right place in every single moment of your existence.

Nothing, - and absolutely nothing - in your existence is left out of the orchestration of your own Divine Self, which is nothing less than an exquisite symphony meant to discover new tones of expressing itself through the time and space continuum.

After all, both light and dark originate from the same Source.

*Scan from right to left*
←

## Recognizing Design Beneath Disorder

*With the power of this name I eliminate the feeling of powerlessness, doubt and fear as I realize the perfection of the universe and the presence of perfect order beneath all apparent disorder.*

# Arrival

Welcome to my kingdom, dear One! I'm the "Queen" of Andromeda and I'm delighted and honored to have been chosen to share my exis-tence with all of you.

This journey you started will go through stages of preparation which will take place at many levels of your being. I was chosen to guide you through the first stage you will encounter, most probably due to a sense of familiarity we are holding in our "kingdom" which resembles your ancient Egyptian culture.

I would like to present to you a set of guidelines which will help you navigate this phase, and avoid big surprises or interruptions in this amazing process.

**No ego** can take charge while in my kingdom. This being your first stop, you may have a tendency to impose or allow (consciously or unconsciously) your ego to rule your actions. We do understand that you may not be aware of it. We are here to help bring it to your awareness. This stage, dear One, is the last stage in which you will encounter your ego at this level of awareness. No one leaves this place unless their ego is in check - meaning "dead", metaphorically speaking. Ego can be revived, but once you realize that it is not serving you when it is expressed at this intensified level, you will allow it to "diminish in intensity". Many of you can't even imagine what an existence will look like without an active and overcharging ego. This stage of letting go of your ego is not to be taken lightly. For some, this could be quite challenging. That is why, at this level, you have the available support of highly compassionate beings. We are not giving up on you, especially after the tremendous work and effort it took to arrive here. We acknowledge and honor your journey.

**Light** will shine through you at a higher intensity now. This happens automatically and will enable you to accelerate your evolutionary process, as well as for those around you as you resonate and radiate more light.

**Rest and Stillness:** This is not a place for doers. There is nothing out there for you to do. Manifestation at this level is beginning to show up instantly, so all you have to do is BE still. So, Be Still!

**Sorority and Brotherhood:** You are here with your family, brothers and sisters, not lovers. What you will experience at this level is not easily comprehensible to many of you. Allow it to be presented to you. It will help if you try remembering the times you were a very young child. Return yourself to that emotional purity in the unity consciousness presented to you at this level.

**Transcendence and Tranquility:** This is the place where you will truly understand the meaning of transcendence, which is to be experienced and expressed in a state of tranquility that many will associate with a sense of "emotionlessness". We choose to call it *emotion expressed at a higher level.* The realization of existence behind your physical body will bring you this state of calmness and stillness as you realize that there is nothing to worry about out there other than your own state of being, which creates everything that exists in your universe, which is the only universe you will ever experience.

**Serenity** is not to be confused with the *tranquility* state, which is the step that comes afterward. Serenity is being experienced by all that exists in your universe. Serenity is achieved at this level, while tranquility is being acknowledged.

**Serendipity or Synchronicity:** Whatever you choose is the theme most experienced at this level.

**Unconditional Love** will begin to be introduced to you in its grandeur, and here you will understand how far you were from knowing it before.

**Knowingness and Oneness** is the profound realization of this level.

Scan from right to left ←

## Great Escape

*With the power of this name, I silence my ego to the
point of relief and therefore achieve freedom from
ego-based desires, views, and selfish actions, thereby
achieving true peace and real fulfillment
in my existence.*

# Asking for Help

We are a collective consciousness from Sirius C constellation, grateful to be of assistance.

Whenever you feel stuck or filled with hatred and despair, surrender to the closest feelings that a child would have in such case. Know that you are never alone and as a child would run to his/her mother, so should you "run" to us for help. Please allow us to come and be of help. We can offer you healing, comfort, peace and compassion.

Please know that you should always ask for help for the Highest Good of All, including your enemies. Remember, we are all in this together. Those are just roles each of us take at times in order for us to learn and TRULY understand.

We are not the only ones coming to help as there are many levels of consciousness assisting you at this time. Know that help will come for each of you from the most appropriate place based on the frequency you are outsourcing at the time.

Do not be concerned about attracting lower or negative frequencies just because you are at that level at the time as this is not what we are saying. Just surrender to the highest form of divinity and ask for help for the Highest Good of All. You can use any wording you wish, but pure positive intention and simplicity is the best way to approach this.

Attracting what you are the frequency of is still a valid law, but *your intention is there to overwrite that.* No matter how low in frequency you are at the time, there is always a door or gate to the highest frequency there is. Know that and use the power of your heart to open that gate. Surrender to its power and not the opposite!

Remember you are never alone, and it is not for your highest good to be alone.

We are all one! Walk your life and mark your dreams knowing that.

*Scan from right to left*

## Absolute Certainty
## in the Light-Force of God

*With the power of this name, I activate my true Faith in God-Source, the Creator of All That Is!*

# Awakening and Awareness

The awakening process is nothing more than anawareness of your dream or existence in the multidimensional space and time.

You were used to seeing yourself at this small level we call "daydreaming". You were also used to believing that all you touch, taste, smell, see, and hear is all that is real or exists. There is nothing falser.

You exist in a multidimensional level in the now and you are not yet aware of it. Only 2% of people who first experience some sort of awakening on Earth can perceive their multidimensionality — and the joke is that many of those who are talking about it have no clue yet about what it truly is.

The true awareness of your multidimensionality will begin its process during the shift. Many of you will experience the shift differently. Reality is perceived in a unique way by each individual Self and therefore this awareness will manifest uniquely from one Self to another.

The awareness of your Self in other worlds can be a fascinating process for your physical mind as you perceive it today. That is why we suggest you move through this part of your journey slowly, so you can enjoy this magic process of rediscovering yourself.

*Scan from right to left*
←

## Prophecy and Parallel Universes

*With the power of this name, I now become aware
of my multidimensionality and the existence
of simultaneous parallel universes
in the NOW present moment.*


*I now understand that I can freely move through an
infinite multitude of parallel universes as I consciously
change my emotional state and choose to vibrate at
certain frequencies. I understand that prophecy is,
in fact a mastery of conscious manifestation.*

# Be and Know Thyself

Arriving at this level took a tremendous effort from You and your Guides. Therefore, the cruelest attitude you can have toward yourself and others at this point is to not *be your true Self*.

Being someoane that others may want or ask you to be will only bring insecurity and powerlessness into your existence. Having to stay in alignment with one-Self moment to moment, brings peace, clarity, serenity, and silence to the mind.

Be whoever you want to be, regardless of the likes or dislikes of others. Be You in the now and find happiness in every moment. Be You and be true to yourself and therefore to others.

You are here now, ready to begin your creation, as is your inner soul's desire. It is only you who can decide what that creation looks like. Be in your truth and eliminate anything else that comes in the way. You can do it beautifully with ease and grace. This is what you prepared yourself for, all along.

Everything you need will surface at the right time.

Be honest with yourself and others. Collect your gifts and pick one to begin with. Any one will do it!

*Scan from right to left*

## Strengthen Spirituality
## for Victory over Addictions

*With the power of this name, I access
a vibrational state of being where I am free
and have successfully overcome all my addictions,
unpleasant behaviors and traits or negative habits.*

# Beginning the Road!

The key to a successful transition is to start "building a road" toward your destination. Indeed, you will have to "build that road" as this is a journey into the unknown and "untraveled land", if you wish to call it that.

*How would I do that?* you may ask yourself. Of course, it will be different for every single one of you, so start asking yourself how you would build a "road"; and where would you build it? You will receive an answer in one form or another.

Doubt is your only enemy at this point. Doubt that you will even have to build that road. What if we tell you that the "road" is not even outside of yourself? You will need to go within and open new doors and territories you never knew existed before. This part of your journey will be a challenging one, dear One.

You must know that you will not be able to advance without your inner child and s/he needs strength to take this journey.

New abilities that we can't even begin to describe will be uncovered by many of you. Have mercy on yourself and do not rush into anything that feels uncomfortable. You are now controlling time and space. Learning to master the manipulation of time and space can be overwhelming at times for many of you. By now, all the knowledge was downloaded into your being, but you do need to go within to access it as it is needed.

We won't tell you that you are the first to do this in this universe. We are, however, saying to you that the possibilities are infinite due to your uniqueness, which will generate new aspects of creation never created before.

The beauty of the present moment will now be truly understood by many!

*Scan from right to left*

## Building Bridges

*With the power of this name, I activate within myself the catalyst connector God-given ability which will allow me to bring peace and serenity within my relationships in this world or between the dimensional worlds.*

# Behind the Veil
*Message from Sananda*

Dear One, you are now in the middle of your ascension process. You are still resisting as you are frightened of the unknown because it was not explained specifically to you what is to be expected.

Go with ease as we are all here supporting every single one of you on all levels and at every depth.

Your reality, beloved One, was there only to help you advance. It was all a game or a movie as you can see it now through those 3D glasses which took you through an illusory trip. Your interaction with it was also illusory, as you could see when you detached yourself from your physical body. Now you understand that your physicality is not who you are in totality. Use your body; cherish it, but do not attach yourself to it. On your new journey, this is the first step you will have to take in order to adapt to your new conditions.

Many of you will increase your conscious astral projections and lucid dreaming. This will become second nature for you, as a walk in the park feels to you now.

You need not work hard at anything but instead, allow it to happen. Breathe Love and have fun!

It is an adventure, after all!

*Scan from right to left*

←

## Angelic Influences

*With the power of this name, I access the positive
divine angelic realm for assistance and guidance!*

# Beloved One!
*Message from Sananda*

We are finally here, as I always knew we would be!

Please take a moment to express your gratitude for all that was and will always be, as all these experiences are nothing else but exactly what you wished for!

Moving forward, we will support you in developing new pathways of existence and adapting to the new one which Mother Earth developed for herself.

As you slide to the new dimension, tremendous changes are occurring on your planet, and not only. You are not to fear these changes as they are bringing out the light and the best in each and every single one of you.

Please allow yourself to go smoothly through these changes so the planet itself won't have to experience unnecessary disturbances.

There is no need for struggling and suffering during this transition. Be with the process and trust that only good will come out of it.

I am here with every single one of you in every form you need me to be. I am at your service entirely and many others as well, with their unconditional love. Nothing can harm you anymore, so unless you want to harm yourself, walk in peace and love.

*Scan from right to left*

## Eliminating Negative Thoughts

*With the power of this name, I recognize
the God ability within myself to transform dark
into light, negativity into positivity and to recognize
that not all thoughts are generated by me and therefore
I have the power and clear discernment to eliminate
the ones I do not prefer.*

# Bliss and Consciousness

Bliss is basically consciousness expressed at higher frequency levels. Once consciousness reaches a limit between two dimensions, the crossing point is experienced as a state of bliss, which differs at each crossing point.

It is like a sign or an award which One is giving to himself/herself to acknowledge and celebrate the evolution of their consciousness.

The challenge is not to get stuck into the bliss state as it can create or attract stagnation in One's evolution. Therefore, once consciousness has reached the bliss point, the next imminent step is crossing over, if we can express ourselves this way.

Many of you can get lost in the "bliss trap" which automatically creates stagnation, imminently followed by a contraction in One's consciousness.

The bliss trap can be as damaging to One's conscious as regression is, on lower levels of consciousness.

So, how can One avoid or prepare himself/herself?

By simply *acknowledging* this truth or introducing it to your awareness. Once you are aware of it, the danger disappears, as it becomes a conscious choice and not a trap anymore.

Enjoy your bliss, dear One and remember to move forward!

*Scan from right to left*

## Unconditional Love

*With the power of this name, I alchemize
the negativity into positivity using the unconditional
love vibration available to me in the NOW.
I use this power to bring harmony
between humanity and the natural world.*

# Chit-Chats of the Universe

**R**esistance: Along the path to your enlightenment there is resistance, which is a natural process of evolution. As dark is to light, there can't be movement without a counter force.

Many of you are dreaming of a better world or dimension where everything is perfect. We are not saying such a world does not exist but, at every level of existence, there is always something which triggers evolution; otherwise, you will experience stagnation which is not a natural way of existence.

Do not confuse this counter force with struggling as life is effortless by its nature, but it keeps evolving and always expanding. Nothing is forever, and everything is in a continuous state of change.

Resistance is, in fact, one key to evolution and expansion. As light is moving through universes, the more resistance it encounters, the more it expands. When you truly understand this at the core of your being, you will realize that resistance will miraculously receive a positive meaning, as everything else in existence truly has.

How can resistance trigger evolution? Naturally, what you resist persists and eventually, resistance will trigger the complete surrender and letting go which is the last step in the mechanics of manifestation. Preceding the complete surrender there is a process of growth and expansion that takes place. Resistance triggers creativity of new patterns and new forms of existence; new beauty to be observed and contemplated. New life is born out of resistance, We are mostly referring to resistance to temptations, abuse, lust, malice, treachery, gluttony, greed and especially desire and attachments.

**Completion** is an illusion of creation. Everything is complete in the present moment — and yet nothing is ever complete, and nothing will ever be complete. This is why every single one of you is creating expansion, generating new forms and new expressions to existence itself. Without you, the existence will be missing something in its infinite creation. Your meaning to creation is evolution.

**Persecution** is a meaning of creation in lower densities. When we persecute someone or yourself, resistance is mainly generated. These practices were the meaning of generating evolution in denser levels of existence, where the danger of stagnation was higher and used by darker forces, which in themselves were stagnating. That is why persecution was allowed, so that resistance could be generated and from there evolution would be placed in motion. Yes, this is an exploration of darkness. After all, how would one appreciate or even perceive light without experiencing the dark? How would one know peace without experiencing war? How would one appreciate love without experiencing hate? The main purpose of 3rd dimensional existence is to experience the extremes and attain the balance.

**Joyful exaltation** is another meaning of creation. It is the other side of the coin as opposed to persecution. In its building blocks is the desire for more and more without the feeling of true fulfilment. Exaltation is meant to "explode" at one point or at a certain level, based on each individual's tolerance. That is why we explain evolution as being not only a claim to a higher level, but also a journey toward your inner core.

Bouncing from one extreme to another is the key to evolution because ultimately, it points you to the center where the ultimate *balance* is found.

*Scan from right to left*

## Passion

*With the power of this name, I access the
true passion of my heart and soul and receive
the strength and wisdom to follow it and act on it
with integrity, devotion, and honesty.*

# Concurring with Your World

Being at ease or in the flow with the present moment will help you be in harmony with your environment and everything that is included in it.

Disagreeing with your environment will create struggling and an increase in that which is not desired.

How can one agree with everything in his/her environment? By simply acknowledging the fact that you are a part of your environment. All that you see or perceive is nothing but a mirror of your inner self, which is in essence an opportunity to better know and understand yourself. Therefore, everything you perceive in every moment is there, at your service.

Everything you perceive is there to serve you in some way as it wouldn't otherwise be perceived by you or even enter your reality. How exactly can it serve you? It is your quest and that is why you call this, "The Game of Life".

All the answers are always inside yourself. How to get the answer? Focus your attention on your heart chakra and give it a gentle touch as you ask yourself why *that something* arrived in your environment. Then try to be aware and listen from a detached place. Ask the question several times if needed and *know* that sometimes it is more effective to ask in writing. To the best of your abilities, always ask the question from a state of curiosity and not despair. If you feel any pain or tension in your body while listening, know that there is fear stopping you from perceiving the truth. It means you got close to a belief or fear whose existence you are threatening. Celebrate!

*Scan from right to left*

## Heaven on Earth

*With the power of this name, I ignite the divine light within myself as guidance of my own transformation and therefore I become a channel for divine creation of a true Heaven on Earth!*

# Conquering the New

Becoming the New is how you start this "business" of conquering the New. We don't mean to sound conceited, although we are aware that this is how some will perceive it at first.

What will happen at this level is a bit different: as you will begin building inside as opposed to building outside of yourself which was a characteristic of a 3rd dimensional experience level.

My name is Anuket and I'm here to begin describing this process to you.

The 3rd dimensional game was showing outside yourself whatever was happening inside yourself; so many expres-sions of the self were refected in the technologies you developed.

Moving forward, the rules are changing: You are now beginning to create and develop those technologies, so to speak, inside yourself, as everything can now be done this way. You desire a time machine, then you become one; you desire a sophisticated computer to do whatever you imagine, then you become one or blend your being with one. Anything you want, you can become as long as you fully embrace it with your entire being. Of course, the matter density is differ-ent in this new dimension, which will make this pro-cess easier and achievable. I desire to express these concepts in a familiar way to allow you to undertake these changes more easily, and hopefully you will have some fun with it while undergoing the process.

I can hear many of you skeptically laughing and asking all sorts of questions. One, in particular, I would love to answer: "How did you, Anuket, start this transition and what did you first choose to become or create in this new dimension?" Now, this is a fine question, and I understand why so many of you will ask it.

Dear One, children of love and light, your deepest desires will manifest in a blink of an eye as you begin to experience freedom from the limitations of 3rd-dimensional existence. I becomes WE and that is what I first experienced. I was everything and everyone at once. I have dissolved into the infinity of this universe and without losing a sense of Self I blended my energy with the other Selves at once. It is hard to describe in words what that explosion of Self did to my awareness.

As I understand, many of you will choose to experience this particular transformation at first, but I want to let you know that this will not necessarily happen to all, not even to the majority. Your deepest desires will become reality for you, in the blink of an eye. Some may desire knowledge, some levitation, and some may desire peace and serenity. You will become and create that in a blink of an eye after which you will move on to wherever your own imagination will carry you.We are all looking forward to those initial creations as they express the heart purity of each and every single one of you.

# Cutting the Edges

There comes a time when a renewal of your "shell" is necessary, unless you are willing to break it off completely, and be without one until you rebuild or grow a new one. You will need to smooth the "blunt edges" as in the process of sharpening a knife.

What "edges" are we talking about here?

Your personality and extrasensory senses are going through a sharpening period. It may not be a very pleasant process as it can be frightening when you may have to let go of some aspects of you which are not useful anymore. Ego is a big one, but until then, some others will prevail.

The best and easiest way to do this is to completely surrender to the process. Remember to always check in with your feelings in your present state.

*Scan from right to left*

←

## Letting Go

*With the power of this name, I achieve true freedom from the past by completely letting go of the ego identities and therefore I am now envisioning and create a future filled with true joy, harmony, and love.*

*I am letting GO of everything NOW!*

# Everything is Self!

Everything in the Universe is a conglomerate of Selves. My Self, his Self, her Self and all the other Selves.

Bringing one Self into consciousness took a tremendous amount of work and dedication. One-Self can't come into existence unless it is embedded with pure Love consciousness. There is no such thing alive which has not pure unconditional love at its core of existence. Acceptance and a deep understanding of this unique truth could resolve all the illusory conflicts which exist now in your dimension.

All that is in existence goes through a cycle of transformation with the drive to return to the One unconditional love and oneness. The closest One-Self gets to the source, the more expansion that Self will experience. Expansion of one-Self triggers the expansion of oneness, which can't ever be reached, but instead is expanded in infinite versions of Self-expansions. That is why Love Oneness is infinite.

There is never an arrival point, but only a new beginning, a new exploration. Expansion of Self triggers the expansion of One, and vice versa.

*Scan from right to left*

## Like Attracts Like

*With the power of this name, I alchemize
the negativity into positivity using the unconditional
love vibration available to me in the NOW.
I use this power to bring harmony
between humanity and the natural world.*

# Expansion

Recall a time when you were watching a balloon being filled with air. Have you observed the way it expands and becomes lighter and lighter? Now, imagine that you are that balloon. Be it! Sense yourself expanding, becoming bigger and bigger, lighter and lighter. Keep your eyes open and focus on one point in front of you. Breathe in through your heart chakra and allow every breath to expand you a bit more.

Allow yourself the sensation of floating, even if illusory. Just let it be like a daydream. Enjoy that feeling of floating in the space around your physical body. This is the beginning step of your elevation process. Expansion of consciousness precedes expansion of physical matter into nonphysical matter. Your transition from the physical to nonphysical involves a lighter stage of your physical matter; a less dense matter, but nevertheless, still matter.

What you are actually doing is expansion. To make it easier for your mind to comprehend this transitional process, please use this analogy of imagining your physical body occupying a larger space. We intend to make this complicated process as simple as possible so you can all enjoy this wondrous journey.

*Scan from right to left*
←

## Defying Gravity

*With the power of this name, I ignite the elevation of
my consciousness by using the power of my higher mind
to elevate my spirit over my physical body and
my soul over my ego. Therefore, I become a more
conscious Creator and my creation expands
and it becomes limitless.*

# Flip Side of Awareness

As you become more aware of certain aspects of yourself, you will automatically access or open a gate to the opposite. In this case, with awareness of the opposite comes the possibility for you to fall deeper into unconsciousness which is the "sleeping mode" of existence.

You will encounter this challenge as you move through the last phase of duality. As you are approaching the limits between the 3rd and 5th dimensional levels up through the 4th transitional dimension, you will be switching from awareness to unconsciousness much more often and more dramatically, if we can express ourselves that way. Do not make it a drama, dear One! It is a good sign, as this is the last phase where all that you are not aware or conscious of must come to the surface to be revealed to your consciousness, processed and integrated into yourself.

This process will be perceived by many to be a difficult one as feelings of powerlessness will arrive when the coin flips to the other side. Dear One, bear with it and do not run from it as this will only make the process more painful. Stay with it and know that we are here, seeing you, holding you, giving you our full assistance. However, we can't do it for you! Before entering this new realm, all must be cleared! Bring it to full awareness and integrate it into who you are. Don't try to diminish or deny any of it. All experiences are yours and have made you who you are. Keep all that you are and know that you have the choice of being who you choose to be by knowing the outcomes of your previous, present and future choices.

You heard us well: You are now being presented with all aspects of who you are on different timelines/dimensions which are in the past or future, although all exist in the Now! We know you have heard this before, as you had to, in order to read this now. Now is the time to actually experience it, which may be challenging for some.

Be aware of this and know that at times, you will lose awareness and that is when you are actually sinking deeper into one aspect of yourself, where the tendency is to completely identify with it. Do NOT, dear One! Do not identify with any of it! Wake up and know that where you are and who you are at a time, is only *one* aspect of yourself. Breathe it in, regardless of your judgment of it as being positive or negative and know that this judgment is also a temporary one.

No experience or role you ever played in the realms of consciousness is a waste. Know that your existence was/is meticulously orchestrated to what was chosen or desired by your expression of All That Is!

As you acquire awareness of all aspects of yourself, you are painting the full picture of All That Is, much like when you would build a puzzle picture. Every single piece of the puzzle is necessary so do not lose any on the way as you cannot enter this realm except in your wholeness.

Therefore, as challenging as it may be at times, or as amazing as it may be at other times, you must integrate it all and move forward until you have collected all the puzzle pieces required to pass through the gate toward the next expression of who you are!

*Scan from right to left*

## Healing

*With the power of this name, I access the limitless
energy of healing at all levels and depths of
my being. I am now radiating that healed frequency
into the world so others can use it, remember it
and reactivate it for themselves.*

# Fruition and Harvesting

As you may sense, this is a time when humanity comes to "fruition". More and more humans are awakening every moment, so it is the "harvest time". This is a time for celebration and enjoyment as well as a time for hard work.

As humans are working during their harvest time to store and preserve the harvest, the same way, we, the parents of humanity, must work to prepare you for your transition journey. You are entering a new stage of your existence completely different from the one you just experienced.

The laws are not the same anymore; everything is changing!

What will become of you?

Well, it depends on what your individuality dictates, but at the same time you will reach a level of Oneness which will blow your mind away if we can express ourselves this way. Individuality completely integrates into the unity.

Our loved One, we are thrilled to experience this transition with you. We cannot express enough of our gratitude for the journey you've done so beautifully.

Many were revealed and no matter what "scars" were acquired during the process, we assure you that all will be healed and that this is what we are here for now.

These healings represent the transition from your physical to the nonphysical. Do not confuse this with the death of your physical body as this is not what we are referring to. As many of you are aware, this transition from one dimension to another is not happening directly, but through a transitional stage which requires these healings that are meant to elevate your being at all levels of its consciousness. *Elevation* is an important stage in this transition, and it implies, of course, raising your frequency and the ability and mastery to maintain it. Many of you are doing this automatically but many will need help. Unity consciousness via these healings is allowing every single being that desires to go through this process of transformation to transcend its obstacles at any level they may reside: physically, mentally, emotionally, spiritually, etc.

Have faith in yourself, allow the process and go with the flow! During this transformational process, every single one of you is being guided and divinely supported in every possible way necessary. You have to ask for assistance if you feel you need it. Just ask once and know that it is given to you instantly.

# God

A vast and complex subject to discuss, but we will keep it simple for now. We only want to reinforce the idea of God or consciousness, so you can create a sturdier foundation to what is to come next.

Simply put: God is consciousness itself which created everything and anything in existence as it expands itself both inward and outward. That is why every single one of you is God and you are all One, the only God consciousness that ever existed.

You are all in a journey of knowing yourself as this is the desire of One consciousness in existence.

All That Is or ever was in existence created the Source which includes all knowledge accumulated from all experiences in existence.

All the struggles and sufferings at individual levels are assisting others for access to the Source and is equally granted to all. We are only mentioning these negatively defined experiences to expand your awareness of your contribution at all times. Do not judge these as negative contributions, because your process to overcome them is a key that others have access to, as you also accessed others' keys at the time you were in need. When you need help all you have to do is ask and that is when you access the Source within, which will grant you what you need at the level you can access in that moment.

How you ask is another story. Ask from your *heart* (feel it), with pure *intention* and no hidden agenda, in the highest good of all, *knowing* and *acting* as if it is already there.

*← Scan from right to left*

## Dialing God

*With the power of this name, I activate*
*my conscious connection with God and therefore*
*I become truly aware of God within myself.*

# Mastering the Art of Creation

**D**ear One, you should not be concerned with the fear of not being able to do it. Creation as you know it in your world is a different concept than creation in this new reality which you are now entering. You were prepared and tested, so there is no need to concern yourself with fears and worries about the future or anything similar. You see, dear One: you wouldn't be here if you would not be able to do it. This is certain!

Concepts and definitions are changing in structure, meaning and complexity. Know you will succeed as long as you are willing to participate. Your unique structure and frequency signature is all that is needed.

Why are we using the word "mastering"? It is because your arrival in this world gives you the right to this title. You are a master, otherwise you could not arrive here. You are ready to enter the true creation floor. You were trained and prepared for this in the illusory simulation of the 3rd dimensional reality and much more.

Your contribution and creation will enrich the Universe. Trust that it is needed and desired by All That Is.

Time has arrived for you to fully involve yourself in the creation of the new Earth. It is time to focus on the "want" instead of what you do not want. Be calm and joyful, trust your power and know that anything is possible. Whatever dreams you have, just allow them to become reality.

Welcome, dear One, and thank you for your gift and presence!

*Scan from right to left* ←

## Global Transformation Begins in Your Own Heart

*With the power of this name, I become aware and conscious of the reflective holographic universe I exist in as I activate and accelerate my own inner transformation toward harmony, peace, serenity and pure unconditional love which exists within my heart.*

# Moving Through Veils of Existence

You probably heard expressions like "singing your way through life", "dancing your way through life" or "dreaming your way through life". Well, dear One, this is what life is: music, a dance or a dream. Flow with it and let it happen. Discover new notes, new steps and imagine and therefore, create new territories.

There is nothing ahead of you which has any consistency, metaphorically speaking, unless you want it to be that way. Move wherever you want to be in the moment, try everything, be everything you wish. Give up on things and paths you don't prefer anymore; move on to another and remember to be playful and joyful.

There is no use in worrying about anything, ever. Remember the blockages are only in your mind and nothing lasts forever. Just keep moving toward what excites you the most and you will find your way through the veils of existence. It is that simple!

*Scan from right to left*

## Thought into Action

*With the power of this name, I activate
a conscious awareness of my thoughts' power
to create the reality I experience and therefore
I now gain complete control over my creation.*

# Parental Choices

We are, in a sense, your parents! As you journeyed through your childhood of existence, we were always with you, watching you, caring for your needs, while allowing you to experience whatever you chose to experience.

As you are approaching maturity, we are slowly letting go of you. This is always challenging on both sides, but what will existence be without that freedom? Imagine living your earthly life with your parents always beside you.

You are now reaching maturity, dear children of light. We are slowly letting go of you so you can shine your splendor and fill us with indescribable joy as you always have done.

There are no wrong choices you can make as there was never a wrong choice that we made with you.

We are always here for you, a thought away, and that is the beauty of our connection.

Never too far and never too close!

*Scan from right to left*

## Divine Umbilical Cord

*With the power of this name, I become conscious of the
eternal umbilical cord which connects me with the Divine
Source and Light. I establish a deeper knowing at all
levels of my being so I can now remember this forever.*

# Participating

Participating in the evolutionary process is a choice and a requirement at the same time. Existence itself requires that. How you choose to do it is dictated by your own free will. Each of you, with no exception, is bringing something new to existence itself. Every contribution is valued the same, regardless of its expression, amplitude, volume, intensity and whatever else can cross your mind as delimitations between those contributions.

In the lower dimensional realms, those so-called "negative expressions" are also helpful. The exploration of darkness makes the opposite possible. The same holds true for the exploration of light, as one cannot be perceived without the other. In this new realm of existence that you are entering, the opposites are merged; so they are, in a way, dissolving into each other.

Your physical mind may not be able to truly understand this now, but know that this new stage of your existence is directly proportional with previous explorations of both: dark and light.

Therefore, dear One, all contributions are equally valuable to the One.

This is not said to encourage negativity and darkness as ONE is pure love at its core. However, because that pure love wants to be seen, it needs a reflection of the opposite so it can be acknowledged and perceived.

You are the One, moving toward an existence in which duality is dissolving; hence, your understanding of the true nature of the ONE becomes much clearer.

*Scan from right to left*

## God is in Charge

*With the power of this name, I am now aware of the God existence everywhere, in everything and everyone.*

*What I put out is what I get back!*
*What I say it becomes!*
*What I believe is what I create!*

# Partnership with God

God is within you and outside of you so how can One partnership with that, you may ask?

You are everything and therefore many things at once as well as nothing, in every single moment.

One may find it difficult to journey through existence being aware of this. One may feel lost at times, which is understandable. However, One needs an in-depth understanding of himself/herself, in order to make this process effortless.

The absence of ego, and therefore the identity loss, may be perceived as challenging at first. Acceptance of who you are and every expression of who you are, in every single moment, is the key to "survival" and thriving on this level. We do not mean survival in the basic sense you may be used to. Allowing All That Is to be expressed through you, it means allowing all that comes into your existence without judgment, resistance or avoidance.

Be kind with yourself. Accept yourself without judgment. Love and create a loving relationship with yourself and others.

The relationship with Self is now a direct reflection of your relationship with God. You are nothing less and nothing more than God.

You are allowed to challenge yourself if you wish, even doubt yourself if you wish, but know that it will only be a waste of your energy as there was never anything constructive nor helpful coming out from that type of relationship.

Be the best partner you could be to yourself. Listen to yourself, be supportive to Your-Self. Do not push or pressure yourself with anything. Give yourself unconditionally. Be there for yourself. Your-Self includes all that you are not just certain identities you chose to express at times-a parent, a profession, inner child, etc.

You are the explorer! You are all that remains after the experience of life itself. You are the wisdom, the kindness, the pain, the joy and peacefulness that remains! You are pure unconditional love at the core of your existence, and you are all that surrounds it at times.

Accept yourself in your wholeness!

# Perceiving the Change

The major transformation Earth and every single one of its inhabitants are going through at this times is being perceived differently at the individual level, and of course by Earth herself.

The planet is in a state of complete forgiveness, and it seems as though she is deeply caring about all that resides on/with her. This is an amazing opportunity for all of you to respond and use her as an example.

Look at this as being an opening - something like a portal - of your planet's magnificent power, which will enhance and ease your process of complete forgiveness.

Please understand that your planet and you, consequently, are undergoing the same process of ascension, and these are challenging times for all of you.

We are deeply moved by this state of forgiveness and peace which arises from the core of planet Earth and affects so much around it.

We sensed several Earth disturbances that vanished and cleared up through the planet's compassionate "tears". We know that many of you can sense this process already; and for those who don't, we encourage you to meditate, focusing and connecting with her empathy using the umbilical cord that exists between your heart and the core of Mother Earth. You will benefit from this process as you will perceive it as being your own, and you will be carried into the heart of it.

Earth is understanding every single one of you, feeling your pains and sorrows and she desires that you also forgive yourself and move behind that past pain. Free yourself from all of the negative thinking and dark expectations. Know that you are deeply loved, and no harm will come to you unless you insist on experiencing it.

Let's breathe together this powerful and peaceful energy. Let us heal ourselves and therefore the world around us.

*Scan from right to left*

## Heaven on Earth

*With the power of this name, I ignite the divine light within myself as guidance of my own transformation and therefore I become a channel for divine creation of a true Heaven on Earth!*

# Perceiving the New

You all keep hearing about this "perception" business lately. Everyone is trying to explain to you how perception is everything, and how the same event appears and is being experienced by each of you based on your own perception, which at times can be very different from what others present at the same time and space with you, are experiencing.

Well, dear One, buckle up! Because it is getting more and more serious now. We mean it, literally serious.

Perception, which is generated by your own unique *belief system*, creates and maintains your *mental, emotional* and *spiritual* state that will eventually induce your *actions* and behaviors, which will ultimately create your world. Again, we mean this literally.

You see dear One, *you are becoming* your world. You are traveling in and out of it. You make it appear and disappear and you are deciding where and what you want to experience and at what level. You are basically creating what you imagine in every split of time and space. So, what you perceive is what you receive, which can also be viewed as what you receive is what you perceived.

Let's dig deeper into this *perception* business...

How do you perceive the Void? Do not say it is "nothing", as nothing in itself doesn't exist and therefore, nothing is *something* and I will immediately ask you how you would perceive nothing. I heard from many describing the Void as a lack or an emptiness, which is similar to "nothing". Others describe it from a space point of view as an echo. Well, whatever it is for you IS what you will experience.

Materiality is, in a way, dissolving before your eyes. Matter will become more fluid at first and then interchange forms, until in time it will disappear before your eyes. Your eyes will perceive things not yet materialized, as if they are already there. You will be playing with space and matter at first, after which you will be playing with time.

You will become some sort of magician in a way as you see it and understand it in the 3rd dimensional reality. Although now, the magic will have no limits.

"Amazing powers!" will surface which will very quickly become a normality to your consciousness. You will be amazed how fast you will become accustomed to it. It is as you always knew it and in a way, it is true. As you are getting closer to the Source which is the place where Spirit resides, you are, in a sense, picking up stronger and stronger the essence of what you are made of.

All that was ever experienced by any being in existence, at any level of its existence is always incorporated into the Source. By you being more aware, much closer to the One, you are now accessing all this data — if we can call it so — much easier and at a higher intensity.

However, duality disappears, if you can perceive that and therefore, everything in existence will automatically include the plus and the minus, the positive and the negative in the same time and space. Therefore, only perception is what delimitates the experience.

Remember, we told you that there is no arrival point, only an infinite series of experiences. The Source is the center and every single creation has the Source at its center/core. Therefore, you are now in this place where everything includes a so-called positive, a negative, and a neutrality or a balance point which is the core of everything in existence.

Let's take an example so you can understand what your heart already knows: Let's say you are in front of a river and contemplate its beauty when a thought crosses your mind and you vividly feel as if the river becomes a force that grows and drowns you. Maybe you are picking up on a memory when your soul at some point in time or in some existence was a body drowned in a river. You allowed the thought, the feeling and therefore you are having this experience in your mind. Is that in your mind only? Is imagination something real? Let me clarify this to you. You cannot imagine something that doesn't exist somewhere! And therefore, you could not have received that thought if it didn't exist somewhere or some time. What is happening here? You are perceiving yourself drowning but you are also perceiving yourself sitting peacefully by the river admiring its beauty. You had a choice about which version you wanted to experience, if any. You choose the most preferred one, always. You have created both realities, but chose one to experience. You are in them and outside of them, at the same time. It is like looking at the same scenery through different windows. In this case, one with a frosty glass and one with a clear glass. You are the eternal One outside of both realities.

What we are trying to say here, dear One, is that you no longer can judge something as being "good" or "bad", positive or negative because both exist at the same time in everything you will ever encounter. It is you who chooses if you want to experience something and if so, what to experience or not to experience,for that matter, as the observer position is the master position after all. All the options ever imagined exist and are equally valid.

In the 3rd dimensional world, you needed to find the balance. Well, *now you are the balance point.* Are you able to wrap your mind around this? Some of you will recognize this process easily as you are the one who chose to be of assistance in this transitional stage you are starting to experience.

Regardless, you will all enjoy it, dear One! We know you will, as we also did!

Scan from right to left

## Freedom

*With the power of this name, I realize life as being joyful and fulfilling as I am moving through existence seeing challenging circumstances as blessings meant to help me with my spiritual transformation and achievement of a true, lasting freedom.*

*Scan from right to left*

← 

## Unity through Sensitivity and Tolerance

*With the power of this name, I remember the ability
to truly see and understand others. I am now seeing
myself as a part of the whole and others
as a reflection of different aspects of myself.
My thoughts and deeds are now reflecting
unity rather than separation.*

# Persisting and Passing

On all levels of our existence there is always a dance between stagnation and advancement.

When stagnation occurs, we keep persisting and making the same choices over and over, claiming that we cannot sense the difference as circumstances were differently "dressed up". However, by persisting this way, it could be seen as a means to our devotion to the evolutionary path. We are willing to go through whatever we must and as many times as it takes to achieve what we come here to achieve.

When we finally overcome whatever there was to overcome, a passing through a lens of light is taking place. Every passing through a lens is embodying you with a specific frequency signature which is unique to your existence. No one can ever carry the same frequency. No one's light can be the same as this passing through is being done in a unique way by every single one of you.

There is no way back through these lenses of evolution as every single passing is changing who you are at the core. It is changing your crystalline structure if we may express ourselves this way.

Dear One, you are passing through several of these lenses at this time. We see you, as we are you. Because of you we are now understanding our own process at an even deeper level, as we see ourselves in you… passing through these lenses of light. It is a beauty and a grandeur difficult to express through words.

*Scan from right to left* ←

## Freedom

*With the power of this name, I realize life as being joyful and fulfilling as I am moving through existence seeing challenging circumstances as blessings meant to help me with my spiritual transformation and achievement of a true, lasting freedom.*

# Platonic Existence

We are using the term "platonic" to give you a bit more of an understanding of what the next level may feel like at first. However, do not take this analogy literally as it does not exactly imply a platonic existence as you define it in your reality right now. However, you may be able to relate to elements of your experience with platonic relationships. It is far from a boring existence, dear One. However, likeness between beings is being expressed in a more platonic way rather than exciting interactions as you may be used to currently.

Excitement is not inexistent, although it is now taking a different expression unknown to you at your current level. You will be living a much more fulfilling life without so many dramatic ups and downs created by your ego. We can say it is a much more balanced or leveled existence but not at all uninteresting. Sexuality is being expressed differently at this level and it has almost nothing in common with what many of you are currently used to. This inner transformation will be unique for everyone, so we cannot really give you step-by-step instructions as everything will be created uniquely by every single one of you. However, one thing we know for sure: relationships will be expressed differently as existence itself vibrates at a higher frequency. Be prepared for that change without making it anything just yet.

Be creative!

*Scan from right to left*

← 

## Happiness

Ask what your soul needs, not what your ego wants.

*With the power of this name, I now have the ability
to recognize and attract true happiness into
my existence instead of selfish ego desires.*

# Pursuing Your Truth

Your existence is filled with a deep desire to pursue your purpose which is mainly an individual perspective on your inner truth. This is the most sacred mission your soul has, and it is always in accordance with the purpose of the Great Soul (Source).

All along you were doing nothing else but looking for that purpose which is nowhere else but hidden in your heart.

Knowing your heart is knowing your purpose, that is why you will always hit a "wall" when you are not honestly following your heart. You are being challenged and tested on this matter on all levels of your existence. Follow your heart, dear One, regardless of what others may say or judge you for.

"How should I do this?" one may ask...

Just keep asking yourself:

> What is truly making me happy?

> What would make me run and laugh exuberantly?

> What would really make my heart jump?

Falling in love is mostly the answer that comes to most of us, and more profoundly, it is happening when we are falling in love with ourselves. Accept yourself with all your flaws and imperfections, being kind with yourself especially when you fail.

Do not judge yourself ever; instead, forgive and understand yourself over and over. That is how you can rise above your imperfections and judgmental attitude toward others.

Know that You Are Great and learn to see the greatness in everything and everyone around yourself.

Be truthful to your feelings and care for that inner child inside yourself. Listen and nurture him/her always.

Be alone with yourself often and try to find and understand your longings. Do not allow a feeling of lack when you discover a desire not yet accomplished or fulfilled. Instead, imagine yourself being the Great God of the Universe and gift yourself that which you desire. See yourself receiving that gift with gratitude, enjoying it, and feeling exuberantly happy. Take your role seriously and generously. Give yourself all that you desire.

That is when you will get to know yourself better and get closer to your inner truth, and therefore closer to the Source.

Enjoy Life!

# Settling into OneSelf

Sitting and striving for more is not the way to be on this new level of your existence. Be the *true you* and you will be exactly what you are meant to be.

Arriving to one point, achieving one goal, getting the power you were striving for, is not the way nor the outcome you are looking for.

Moving your perspective from a static point of view to a continuous change of perspective and therefore environment is how you will be living on this new level of your existence.

Being an empty vessel at all times and in every moment of your existence is the only way. Nothing fills you and nothing stays, everything moves into you and through you. It comes and goes, leaving you empty and yet fills you.

Dear One, you will understand it once you experience it. This part is not one that can be taught and it is not our intention to teach you but to bring it to your awareness, as there is no right or wrong way to approach this level.

Trying to guess what is at the next level is not the best way to approach this, either. This is the only reason we felt compelled to guide you in this way. It was different for us and you are changing this.

Speeding up the process is not our intention, either Our pure intention is only to smooth out the process and nothing more as we don't desire to interfere in your process.

Proceed with trust, love, and excitement!

*Scan from right to left*
←

## Listening to Your Soul
Remove limitations to cross your personal Red Sea

*With the power of this name, I enhance a clear communication with my soul.*

# Sinking into Your Truth Reality

Completing this part of your journey will take you deeper into your own idea of truth; your own truth reality.

This trip can be a scary or an enjoyable one, depending on your perspective and approach. What is it that scares you the most? Being seen? Being alone and unloved? Being powerful and not being able to assess your responsibilities? What are the beliefs that hold you back? Sink into them at a deeper level than you ever sank before, and you will be able to conceal this phase of your existence beautifully. Do not let anything frighten you, do not let anything stop you from discovering the greatness, which was always there, deeply hidden inside your heart. Allow the process and do nothing but observe yourself. Observe the frightened you, observe the excited child within you, observe the fear and terror, the beauty and the greatness. Know that you will always surface no matter how deep you sink into the sea of your own truth reality.

This, dear One, encapsulates this part of your existence and this part of your journey can be concealed now. Download your personal symbol and have a wonderful journey ahead!

Love and Joy!

P.S. Your personal symbol is a symbol embedded in your energetic DNA and can be downloaded in any way you wish. To access it, meditate, just draw what you sense or look around you as you may have already downloaded it, or it may be hanging in your room. It could be a simple symbol you love drawing, a picture, or a sign. You will know when you find it! The download of your personal symbol signifies the transition from one evolutionary phase to the next and therefore this symbol cannot be downloaded before you are ready to complete your current evolutionary phase.

*← Scan from right to left*

## Sharing the Flame

*With the power of this name, I access the strength and integrity I need to share throughout the world, the divine pure Light and Joy within my heart as reflected in my thoughts, words, and deeds.*

# The Eternal You

You exist and you will always exist amidst everything. Something in you will always wake up to realize this truth.

Make your way through the river of life by blending your energy with it.

You are the one creating everything that has ever touched your existence.

Begin by being aware of your thoughts at all times. Consciously or unconsciously, your mind has created all that exists in your life. Journey through life with more awareness of your energy and your perception of reality by consistently questioning yourself:

- What meaning do I give to circumstances in my reality and why;

- Am I being completely honest with myself?

- Are you sure you are not avoiding something or disguising it in a different form in order to hide it from your conscious awareness?

- Are you showing your true self, or you are wearing a mask?

Be aware and do not fear yourself. Go deeper and deeper into yourself, and undress each thought and emotion you encounter. Feel it and inquire into it.

Make a conscious decision to be yourself and live your life being true to yourself. Don't cry inside while placing a fake smile on your face, as this will be perceived as disingenuous." Be honest with yourself always! This is the only way you can achieve true fulfilment.

Love always!

*Scan from right to left*

## DNA of the Soul

Bring order into your life by connecting to your soul

*With the power of this name, I bring order, clarity and meaning to my life creation!*

# The Beginning

Light is the secret universal key. Light is the One.

A complete identification with the light can be achieved through complete discipline and control of your thoughts, emotions, speech and action. A complete calmness is also essential. Peace and gnosis will follow.

The secrets of alchemy were kept hidden for the time during the sleeping stage of humanity. The power that resides behind its techniques was not allowed to be seen nor revealed to those not yet ready or those who threatened the universal balance.

The awakening of humanity made the sharing of universal secrets now possible, so its tools and techniques will help humanity elevate to the next evolutionary level.

Today you should begin downloading the symbol that will help you open the entrance to the hallway of this transformational process.

Close your eyes and breathe to achieve a gamma state as follows: Open your mouth and inhale through the mouth directly into your throat. Exhale the same way. Breathe deeply and regularly. Now close your mouth and keep the same breathing directly into your throat as if your mouth were open. You will know when you are in the gamma state. In this state, with the intention of seeing or sensing the symbol, you will receive it. It may be a complicated one, or as simple as a circle. This is an individual symbol for your unique journey. Draw it, write it down and place it in a visible place around your space where you spend the most time. Downloading this symbol may take up to 48 hours, or you may receive the nudge to let it go for now.

After you receive it, focus on keeping your heart chakra open, and trust. No resistance and no doubt should exist in that moment. Visualize it and let it take you wherever it wants to take you.

Once you enter the hallway, know that many will enter but not all will go farther. There is no judgment here. Trust your feelings and know that you will always be exactly where you need to be and you will always receive exactly what you need, when you need it.

The first perception after entering will be that of the dark as that is what needs to be penetrated inside yourself. Be gentle with yourself and imagine entering your heart chakra from the back, and as you pass through it, it becomes a concentrated light which comes out through the front with an explosion of bright, golden yellowish light. That light is now illuminating the hallway. What do you perceive now? Follow the path, wherever it takes you. Trust!

*Scan from right to left*

←

## Prophecy and Parallel Universes

*With the power of this name, I now become aware*
*of my multidimensionality and the existence*
*of simultaneous parallel universes*
*in the NOW present moment.*

*I now understand that I can freely move through an*
*infinite multitude of parallel universes as I consciously*
*change my emotional state and choose to vibrate at*
*certain frequencies. I understand that prophecy is,*
*in fact a mastery of conscious manifestation.*

Scan from right to left

## Strengthen Spirituality
## for Victory over Addictions

*With the power of this name, I access
a vibrational state of being where I am free
and have successfully overcome all my addictions,
unpleasant behaviors and traits or negative habits.*

# The Light

The Light is the Universe's secret key. Light is the One.

For human consciousness, a complete identification with the Light can be achieved in absolute serenity through discipline and utter control of thought, speech and action.

The first step in achieving this elevation is through silence, peace, and knowingness!

The secrets of alchemical transformation were kept secret and safe for a long time during the sleeping time of humanity as the power residing behind its techniques was not safe in the hands of the dark lower consciousness.

The awakening of humanity now makes it possible for us to share tips and techniques which can help humanity elevate to a higher consciousness.

As you start your journey keep in mind that the wellness of your physical body is important. Clean air, water, food and light are essential for your physical body during your ascension process.

It is crucial that you eliminate the dead and dense foods from your diet. Meat, for instance, has a dense frequency which may indeed provide you with some minerals but densifies your structure. Fish is easier on the body-spirit complex, as you may sense that fish flesh is many times still alive as you prepare it, even after hours of being out of its natural environment. However, do not use it excessively and avoid bottom-feeder shellfish.

We strongly encourage you to respectfully bless and thank every spirit that provides you with its body. Clean your water before drinking it. You don't need sophisticated machines or filters as your simple conscious focus and intent will do it. Eat higher vibrational foods and avoid nightshade vegetables as much as possible. Fruits have the highest vibration on Earth as they are offered by nature and are more beneficial when ingested on their own, on an empty stomach.

You are children of the Sun so ease your way through the ascension journey by ingesting sun-growing vegetables and fruits. Avoid or reduce night-shades vegetables.

As you step into this new era, wondrous doors will open for you. Keep an open mind and walk cautiously. Use certain symbols we sent to you as those will help you ease the process. The symbol of fruition, for example, which you call the Flower of Life, is a powerful one to use along your journey.

# The Glitters

My journey was once like yours is today. We all mingle through the days and nights as stars in the earthy sky.

The purpose of these journeys is nothing else but the discovery of Self. The Self is the key to evolution.

The passing of the eons of self-discoveries are enriched by the eons of reverse travelings below. This may not make sense to some of you, so we believe we should attempt to elaborate this just a bit.

You are probably familiar with the phrase "as above so below" and now we would like you to associate that concept with other concepts such as: inside vs. outside, forward vs. backward — as these are exactly the same idea and have no different meaning whatsoever. Expansion is spherical.

The idea of evolution does not mean always going ahead or being above, but it also means going backwards or below. Evolution cannot exist if the motion is always in one direction, forward or above.

In regard to this, we want to introduce to you the idea of "glittering". Don't fool yourself by associating the motion of moving forward with evolution. A true evolution is a constant motion between two opposites which is a process that cannot ever be stopped. That is why evolution on one level, whatever that level may be – above or below – automatically triggers evolution on the opposite level. You may have heard the expression: "You will find your light at the bottom of your darkness". That is why the "dark night of the soul" precedes ascension to a higher level of consciousness.

Now you may understand why we are so eager to be of assistance with your unique journey of self-exploration.

*Scan from right to left*

←

## Dream State

*With the power of this name, I bring meaning to my dream state so I can travel in realms which help me with my evolution and challenges I currently encounter in this reality. My dreams are now clear, more lucid, and prophetic.*

# The Joy of Living

You *must,* dear One, discover and embrace the TRUE joy of living.

As you are coming out of the "dark night of the soul", this task may feel almost impossible and challenging to achieve at first. Rest assured and know you will soon overcome this difficulty.

We are always watching and guiding you, and we are closely tracking your improvement and growth.

You are doing just fine!

*Scan from right to left*
←

## Absolute Certainty
## in the Light-Force of God

*With the power of this name, I activate my true
Faith in God-Source, the Creator of All That Is!*

# The Truth Shall Set You Free

There is no such truth comprehendible to everyone, but rather an individual expression of it.

"All That Is" is also an individualization of every entity that exists. To be with the One requires to be the One. All is included in and outside the One. Every perception is required to realize the One and to include the One as well as to be in the One.

There is nothing disconnected from the One as it never, ever was. We lower ourselves into the unknown to perceive into One much deeper.

Your truth is what you decide to perceive and give power to. Allow yourself to sink deeper into your own perceptions and see how far it will take you. We are looking forward to anything which will be unveiled, anything! Nothing has lesser importance than anything else.

Your journey is unique and will unveil to you, and only to you for now, what is deeply seeded inside the One of your own unique perception. This is not a play on words but rather a revealing of your own truth. Sink deep into it and surrender to its peace and serenity. Our love is with you always!

*Scan from right to left*

## Courage to Speak Your Mind/Tell the Truth

*With the power of this name, I now have the strength and ability to eloquently speak the truth and always speak from my heart.*

# Tips and Clues

Access the power within, it is always there!

Remember life is a game and refections of your inner world are manifesting in your outer world. Watch your environment and others. Accept and take responsibility for your part in those reflections and dance with the one you prefer. Heal or drop the one you don't prefer.

Always trust where you are as being the most perfect and appropriate place to be.

Acknowledge and be grateful for your evolution. Trust your path always!

When you get upset about certain circumstances, you are maintaining and enforcing the negative outcome of the experience. The best way to overcome the unpreferred circumstance is to acknowledge it, understand to the best of your abilities why you attracted it through an honest inner inquiry, ac-cept it, then take an action to the best of your abilities to remedy the situation. Only then will the Universe meet you unexpectedly and support you uncondi-tionally by giving you a hand in better understand-ing the lesson contained. As a result, the unpreferred outcome will miraculously disappear. Remember that a lesson once learned at the core level will vanish from your reality as there is no need for you to repeat a lesson already learned.

Persist but do not insist!

Remember that a wise way to live life is by choosing the effortless path, always. After all, life is a *dance, not a push!*

*Scan from right to left*

## Thought into Action

*With the power of this name, I activate
a conscious awareness of my thoughts' power
to create the reality I experience and therefore
I now gain complete control over my creation.*

# Tools You are Carrying with You

We would like to help you take an inventory of some tools you are carrying on this journey to the next expression of your existence.

**The Light** is who you are and that in itself is the most valuable and important tools of all. We know you have heard what light is, but have you really understood what it is that you truly are?

What is first coming to your consciousness when you are envisioning light? Is it warm in your heart right now? If so, feel that warmth. What does it feel like? Pleasant, perhaps? Like love, maybe? Would you say that light feels like love? Let's try this way: Imagine love in your heart. Does it feel warm? I bet it does. The more you focus on it, the more it fires up. It can eventually explode into a bright white light.

Light is at the core of every single being in existence. Light is what defines everything and every single one of you. Replace the word with love and hopefully you will now understand why love heals everything and why love will always bring you home.

Use your light wisely when falling into the abyss of your own existence!

# Mind and Thought - Creativity

This is a tool you are carrying with you, so you can manifest that love into whatever your mind is able to imagine. It is like a super organic computer which will create whatever was intended but be aware: it has no power on its own as you are the one who gives it life.

Be aware that a thought, once created, cannot be taken back. It is out there expressing that which it was intended in a blink of an eye.

If you are here, it means you had your training, so you passed the tests and therefore you are mastering your thought already. However, we must remind you the key word is *responsibility*. Be aware of your response-ability and use it wisely.

You cannot create or attract anything else except what is inside yourself.

You have and will continue to clear negativity until you fully enter that territory of exploration which we call existential abyss: the Void, as many of you call it.

Many clearings are required before you can enter, and you are being assisted at many levels by higher consciousness beings.

Your ego, dear One, is not necessary on that level so you will have to let it go before entering the abyss. It won't be hard if you don't make it hard!

Everything is changing on the next level. No more separation and no more illusions. Illusion was a necessary tool in your training program only.

We love you and we excitedly await our reunion!

*Scan from right to left*

← 

## Cleansing Hatred from the Heart

*With the power of this name, I clear all negativity from my heart and consciousness so the pure unconditional love from the core of my heart can now be revealed.*

*Scan from right to left*
←

## Freedom

*With the power of this name, I realize life as being joyful and fulfilling as I am moving through existence seeing challenging circumstances as blessings meant to help me with my spiritual transformation and achievement of a true, lasting freedom.*

# Transcending the Illusion

In the beginning, if there ever was a beginning, was the illusion of emptiness, darkness, and Void. We all transcended that and now we find ourselves having a hard time transcending the illusion of what lies in front of our physical eyes.

All that we created started in our imagination. So, what is imagination? Could it be a download from another dimension? A parallel reality, perhaps?

What is real? Some will say that reality is what you can touch. Then why would you believe anything shown on your TV screens even if it is something you are seeing for the first time? Others will say that reality is what can be proven scientifically. What about the double slit experiment then? Couldn't imagination be the same? You are the magnificent Creator, and anything can be created. Why would you limit yourself in creating something that was created before? What is the fun in that? Why would you limit yourself to what you see and not reach for what you can imagine?

Some others will say: You can imagine anything you want as long as what you imagine is something doable. What is doable? Something that respects the universal laws? Universal laws are supporting anything and anyone as long as the creator understands that which is created is always returning to its creator. You, as well, are also on a journey which will end up back to the Creator or Source as many are calling it. Why wouldn't you bring your unique contribution to the Creation? Why would you limit your creation?

Be magnificent and know that whatever road you decide to take is OK and you will receive full and unconditional support all along. You are never alone, and you never were. Being alone was also an illusion.

Close your eyes and focus on your inner heart. Breathe deeply and comfortably. Let your mind wander or imagine whatever it wants. Don't judge anything and don't be afraid of anything. Be free and just allow your imagination to wander freely. What do you sense or see? Start your journey there and keep going! See where it takes you!

*Scan from right to left*

←

## Miracle Making

*With the power of this name, I overcome the self-centered mentality and all negative behaviors and therefore initiate the power of synchronicity and miracles into my life.*

# You are the Midst of Your Own Universe!

You are the center of your universe as everyone else is the center of their own universe.

This is the key or core of multidimensional holographic realities — the universe you are experiencing. The interconnectedness, in itself, is the structure of All That Is. Therefore, you could say that All That Is represents a multitude of interconnected realities. Being the center of your universe means being the center of All That Is, which can give you a perspective of your greatness and your power. This power should only trigger the magnificent responsibility you carry onto yourself and into your own existence.

Your universe is the only universe that will ever exist for you. From your perspective, there is no other universe. Your universe is your "kingdom". There is nobody else making the rules in your universe or manifesting something without your permission at some level.

Your universe has multidimensional levels or parallel realities. Your consciousness is the only center of that universe and it is all that exists in that universe. Anything you attract into that universe is interconnecting with your universe for only one purpose: For you, to know yourself!

Everything is playing by your "rules" as this is your own universe, and you are the only one in control of it. That is why you are always safe, and nothing is ever being done to you without your approval at some level, be it consciously, unconsciously, higher self level, soul, oversoul level, and so on.

Your universe is nothing but a reflection of your own consciousness which is who you are and therefore everything in your universe is nothing but consciousness.

All the others with whom you are interrelating are nothing else but reflections of your own consciousness who are respecting the rules of your "kingdom", rules which are created by the highest level of your consciousness to serve the main goal for which this universe was originally created: To Know Thyself!

*Scan from right to left*
← 

## Lost and Found

Wisdom to find, and not lose sight of direction

*With the power of this name, I find and remember my center and true power of the Creator that I AM.*

## You are the One!

On the breaking edge of ages there is always a rush toward reaching the end or arriving to a certain destination. It is the illusion of separation which creates this nudge in One's consciousness.

We are working on alleviating that urge "to get there" because you can never be anywhere else but where you belong in each and every single moment of your existence. You will not be left behind, and you are not less, nor more than anybody else. You are all working together, always! You are the One and part of the One!

You are the sphere, its center and its edges, all at the same time.

You are including it, and it is including you!

*Scan from right to left*

## Sharing the Flame

*With the power of this name, I access the strength and integrity I need to share throughout the world, my true divine Light and Joy which exists within my heart as reflected into the world through my thoughts, words, and deeds.*

# About the Author

Zouza Wakinyan - healer, channeler and spiritual teacher was always a seeker of her true divine purpose on earth. Following the apex or of her awakening experience, she discovered a deep-seated desire to help end the suffering of humanity, utilizing what she calls "miraculous energy-frequency healing techniques". Zouza realized that these healings trigger a transformational journey of the individual, with direct effect on the spiritual evolution of humankind!

Her research led her to books like "The Book of Knowledge - The Keys of Enoch" and into researching the secrets of kabbalah . Later, she was called to esoteric healing techniques such as those performed by the master teacher Joshua.

Zouza was born and raised in a small village in Northern Romania during the communist regime in a strong and independent family. Growing up with a powerful connection to Mother Nature, she learned the secrets of sustainable farming, herbalism, and ancient wisdom passed down through generations

Zouza describes how her skeptical and forthright personality has been humbled and forever changed by a series of esoteric experiences of which she never dreamed possible. These began with vivid out-of-body experiences and telepathic communication with what she later learned to be the Arcturian light beings. This continued with daytime visions, plant and sun communications, astral-wormhole travel, lucid dreaming, and many other experiences that helped her to understand the undeniable truth that we are never alone and the connection with the spiritual realm is real and accessible to everyone. She was taught about the mechanics of creation, the nature of reality, cosmic mirroring, meditation, astral travel and how to further connect with the higher realms by using different techniques including automatic writing and channeling, which is how this book was born.

The messages in this book were received subsequent to her awakening over the course of three months during her spiritual transformation process from proverbial caterpillar to butterfly. At first the messages seemed rather fictional and nonsensical to her practical mind, but she later learned about the energetic component of these messages and began to receive confirmation regarding the validity of these transmissions.

Although the messages were originally written for assistance with her own transformational journey, she felt compelled to share so that others could also benefit from the information transmitted by these light beings, who revealed themselves as future versions of our current humanity.

You can find more about the author at
**www.reconnectionnext.com**

## Appreciation

*With the power of this name, I access the infinite abundance from Source and bring it into this present moment and embodiment from which I am emanating a state of abundance and appreciation for myself and everything else with a deep sense and knowing that I am enough as I am Now.*

Made in the USA
Columbia, SC
13 November 2022

70804465R00065